BiG Thoughts for Little Thinkers

THE TRINITY
BY JOEY ALLEN

New Leaf Press

First Printing: March 2005
Second Printing: March 2007

Copyright © 2005 by Joey Allen. All rights reserved.
No part of this book may be used or reproduced in any manner
whatsoever without written permission of the publisher, except in the case of brief quotations in articles and reviews.
For more information write:
New Leaf Press Inc., PO Box 726, Green Forest, AR 72638
Illustrations and text by Joey Allen

For my wife Christy

ISBN-13: 978-0-89221-614-7
ISBN-10: 0-89221-614-X
Library of Congress Control Number: 2004118190
Printed in Italy

FOREWORD

Today, it is strange to find an interest in doctrine or theology. Many wish to focus on experience or feeling and think that doctrine blunts the sharpness of both. Others think that theology detracts from the devotional life, from a warm, authentic relationship with God in the heart. Such people have lost sight of the truth that *faith* is the root of all things spiritual. Actually, that's all doctrine and theology are — expressions of what we as Christians ought to believe. Faith is a virtue, the foundational virtue to a relationship with God. We come to God and remain with Him by means of our faith.

Joey Allen, thankfully, has not forgotten this. His heart and his head overflow with faith. He is convinced of the centrality of doctrine and the virtue of faith for every person, young and old. In this helpful, practical, simple, engaging, enjoyable, and trustworthy book, he leads adult and child alike into faith — the joy of believing the truth about God. I smile and see more clearly each time I open up Joey's words and illustrations. I think you will too.

– Dr. D. Jeffrey Bingham

Department Chair and Professor of Theological Studies

Dallas Theological Seminary

A WORD TO PARENTS AND TEACHERS

The doctrine of the Trinity is one of the most important Christian teachings in the entire Bible. It teaches us about the nature of God himself, the Ultimate Reality. Our children need to be taught about God because our actions flow from our ideas about God.

This book attempts to summarize some of the most foundational Christian beliefs — beliefs that have been held by all Christians for the last 2,000 years. No attempt has been made to create new teachings, but simply to pass on to the next generation "the faith which was once for all delivered to the saints" (Jude 3).

Every illustration of the Trinity falls short of adequately describing God. Nothing from the created world can fully illustrate God because He is the Creator. Therefore, this book does not compare God to an egg or the sun or any created thing, but rather credits children with the ability to accept true statements about God by faith. Children have a huge capacity for faith (Matthew 18:3). We should use teachable moments wisely.

In the back of this book, you will find the Constantinopolitan Creed of A.D. 381 quoted in full. The Constantinopolitan Creed, often called the Nicene Creed, provides us with a

summary of orthodox (i.e., correct) Trinitarian teaching that has been accepted and believed by Christians through the ages. The Creed uses precise language in order to correct misunderstandings and false teachings about God. The early creeds that were received by the whole church serve as priceless tools that guide us as we seek to understand God and explain Him to our children.

My prayer is that this book will draw children closer to the Lord and enable them to worship Him in spirit and truth.

– Joey Allen

Hi! My name is Angel. I want to tell you about God. No one is more important or more wonderful than God.

Psalm 136; 145:3; 1 Timothy 1:17

God is holy. That means that He is different from anyone you know.

Psalm 99:3, 5, 9; Isaiah 6:3; 1 Peter 1:16

God is good. He is perfect. Sometimes we do bad things. These are called sins. God never sins. He never does anything mean or bad.

Deuteronomy 32:4; Luke 18:19; James 1:13

God is happy! God is not lonely, and He does not need anything.

Job 41:11;
Psalm 50:12; 135:6;
Acts 17:24-25

God is everywhere. Even though you cannot see Him, He hears your prayers.

*Psalm 139:7-12; Jeremiah 23:23-24;
Matthew 6:5-6; Acts 17:28; 1 Timothy 6:16*

God knows everything. He knows what happened yesterday, what is happening right now, and what will happen tomorrow.

Psalm 90:2; 139:1-6;
Isaiah 46:10; Hebrews 13:8

God knows your name. He even knows how many hairs you have on your head!

Isaiah 43:1; Matthew 10:30

God made everything. No one made God. He never had a beginning, and He will never have an end. He was here before the world began.

Isaiah 40:28;
Revelation 4:8, 11; 22:13

God created the whole world. God made the sun, and the trees, and even my kitty!

Genesis 1:1–31; Isaiah 45:18; Amos 4:13; Acts 14:15

There is only one God. He is in control of the whole world. He has all the power.

Psalm 115:3; Isaiah 45:21–22; 46:5–11; Matthew 19:26; 1 Corinthians 8:4; 1 Timothy 1:17

There is only one God, but God is three persons: the Father, the Son, and the Holy Spirit. They are different from each other, but each one is God. This is called the Trinity.

Genesis 1:26;
Psalm 110:1; Isaiah 48:16; 63:10;
Matthew 28:19; 2 Corinthians 13:14;
1 Peter 1:2; Jude 20-21

The Trinity cannot be completely explained because God is not like anything in the world. God is greater than we can ever imagine.

Isaiah 55:9; Romans 11:33

The Father, Son, and Holy Spirit live united as one God. The Trinity teaches us how to live in unity with different people.

Deuteronomy 6:4; 1 Corinthians 12:4–7; Ephesians 4:4-6

Because God is Trinity, God has never been lonely. God did not create us to be alone either. We need other people. You can't even play leapfrog if you are by yourself!

Genesis 2:18; John 17:5, 24;
1 Corinthians 12:14-31

God gave us the Bible so we could know and believe in Him. We can trust what the Bible says because it came from God, and God never lies.

Numbers 23:19; Psalm 119:105;
2 Timothy 3:16; Titus 1:2

od loves you. God loves all the people in the world. He created us to be close to Him, but our sin separates us from God. The bad things we do come from our sinful hearts. We deserve to die because we are sinners.

Isaiah 59:2;
Ezekiel 18:4;
Romans 3:10; 5:8

God has a solution to our problem! God the Father sent His Son to be born as a baby. They named Him Jesus.

Isaiah 7:14; John 1:14; 3:16;
Galatians 4:4-5; Philippians 2:5-11

Jesus is completely God and completely human. Even though Jesus is God, He became like us, but He never sinned.

John 1:1-3; Colossians 2:9; Hebrews 1:3; 4:15

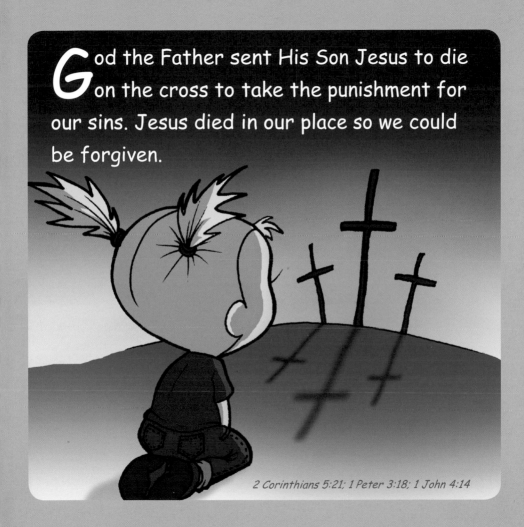

After Jesus died on the cross, He was buried. Then, on the third day, Jesus came back to life! Jesus is alive, and He wants to give you eternal life!

Mark 16:6; 1 Corinthians 15:3-7

Eternal life is a free gift to everyone who trusts in Jesus. Jesus took our punishment when He died so that we could live with Him forever!

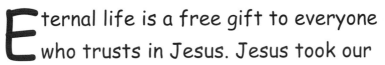

Romans 6:23; Ephesians 2:8-9; Titus 3:5

Jesus is alive, and He will give you eternal life if you believe in Him. The Holy Spirit will begin to change you into the kind of person God created you to be!

Acts 16:31; Galatians 5:16, 25

The Holy Spirit teaches you how to pray and understand the Bible. He helps you love and serve other people.

Romans 8:26; 1 Corinthians 12:4-11

When you believe in Jesus, you will become a child of God. God will be your Father, and He will never let you go!

John 10:28-29;
1 John 5:13

Thank you for letting me tell you about God. I hope you have fun learning more about God.

THE CONSTANTINOPOLITAN CREED OF A.D. 381

We believe in one God, the Father All Governing, creator of heaven and of earth, and of all things visible and invisible;

And in one Lord Jesus Christ, the only-begotten Son of God, begotten from the Father before all time, Light from Light, true God from true God, begotten not created, of the same essence as the Father, through Whom all things came into being; Who for us men and because of our salvation came down from heaven, and was incarnate by the Holy Spirit and the Virgin Mary and became human. He was crucified for us under Pontius Pilate, and suffered and was buried, and rose on the third day, according to the Scriptures, and ascended to heaven, and sits on the right hand of the Father, and will come again with glory to judge the living and dead. His Kingdom shall have no end.

And in the Holy Spirit, the Lord and life-giver, Who proceeds from the Father, Who is worshiped and glorified with the Father and Son, Who spoke through the prophets; and in one, holy, catholic, and apostolic Church. We confess one baptism for the remission of sins. We look forward to the resurrection of the dead and the life of the world to come. Amen.

Also available in this series:

ISBN: 0-89221-615-8

ISBN: 0-89221-617-4

ISBN: 0-89221-616-6

Available at Christian bookstores nationwide

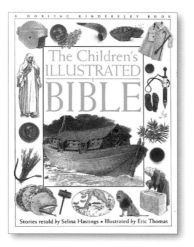